Adult Bible

Concise Commentary
Fall 2021

Adapted from *The Basic Bible Commentary series*

ADULT BIBLE STUDIES CONCISE COMMENTARY FALL 2021

Adapted from the *Basic Bible Commentary,* copyright © by Graded Press, an imprint of The United Methodist Publishing House.

Editor: Rachel Hagewood
Writers: Edward P. Blair; Robert H. Conn; Lynne M. Deming; Linda B. Hinton; Orion N. Hutchinson, Jr.; Earl S. Johnson, Jr.; Frank Johnson; Robert E. Luccock; Norman P. Madsen; James E. Sargent
Designer: Matt Allison

Print Version:
ISBN: 9781791021467
PACP10598775-01

ePub Version:
ISBN: 9781791021474

21 22 23 24 25 26 27 28 29 30—10 9 8 7 6 5 4 3 2 1

MANUFACTURED IN THE UNITED STATES OF AMERICA

FALL 2021

OUTSIDE IN

Introduction to the Unit

A sense of community and belonging are essential emotional connections that people need to thrive. Sociologists studying the story of the early church often attribute the growth of the church to the sense of belonging that it offered people in a world where belonging was limited to those with things such as property, high status, and/or birthright. This unit looks at the various ways that the Bible makes clear how we belong to God's people, even when we appear to be outsiders.

September 5, 2021

Lesson 1
HOSPITALITY TO STRANGERS

Focal Passage
Jeremiah 29:4-14

Background Text
Jeremiah 29:1-23

Purpose
To explore how to live out God's call to show hospitality to the "strangers" in our lives

Summary
Throughout the Books of Exodus, Numbers, Leviticus, and Deuteronomy, God reminds the Israelites that, beginning with Abraham, they have been foreigners, living among people who resided in Canaan and then Egypt. Once they enter the land that God is giving them, God expects them to show hospitality to other resident foreigners. In Babylon, the Israelites have once more become aliens in a foreign land, but now God encourages the people in exile to experience God's shared vision of well-being for all people by extension of their working for the welfare of Babylon.

SCRIPTURE
Jeremiah 29:4-14

⁴The LORD of heavenly forces, the God of Israel, proclaims to all the exiles I have carried off from Jerusalem to Babylon: ⁵Build houses and settle down; cultivate gardens and eat what they produce. ⁶Get married and have children; then help your sons find wives and your daughters find husbands in order that they too may have children. Increase in number there so that you don't dwindle away. ⁷Promote the welfare of the city where I have sent you into exile. Pray to the LORD for it, because your future depends on its welfare.

⁸The LORD of heavenly forces, the God of Israel, proclaims: Don't let the prophets and diviners in your midst mislead you. Don't pay attention to your dreams. ⁹They are prophesying lies to you in my name. I didn't send them, declares the LORD.

¹⁰The LORD proclaims: When Babylon's seventy years are up, I will come and fulfill my gracious promise to bring you back to this place. ¹¹I know the plans I have in mind for you, declares the LORD; they are plans for peace, not disaster, to give you a future filled with hope. ¹²When you call me and come and pray to me, I will listen to you. ¹³When you search for me, yes, search for me with all your heart, you will find me. ¹⁴I will be present for you, declares the LORD, and I will end your captivity. I will gather you from all the nations and places where I have scattered you, and I will bring you home after your long exile,[a] declares the LORD.

---

[a] Jeremiah 29:14 Or *I will restore you to the place from which I exiled you.*

COMMENTARY
Jeremiah 29:4-14

Chapter 29 continues the reports of Jeremiah's confrontations with religious leaders. The leaders named in this chapter are exiles living in Babylon. Messages are exchanged between those people left in Jerusalem and those in exile. These letters are carried by royal couriers (verse 3) or by other travelers (see Ezekiel 33:21). To travel between Jerusalem and Babylon took from four to six months.

Letter to the Exiles

The king's messengers take a letter from Jeremiah to the exile community living in Babylon. Zedekiah is perhaps sending his envoys to Nebuchadnezzar to assure the Babylonian king of his continued loyalty in the aftermath of possible plans for rebellion (see Jeremiah 27:3). Zedekiah himself visited Babylon in 593 B.C. (see Jeremiah 51:59). This visit may have been required by Nebuchadnezzar to reaffirm Zedekiah's loyalty to him. Some of the Israelite exiles may have been involved in the rebellion or in encouraging rebellion against Nebuchadnezzar in 595–594 B.C. (verses 7-8, 21).

King Jeconiah (verse 2) is Jehoiakim, who is still called the king of Judah by the Babylonians. His imprisonment by Nebuchadnezzar may have resulted from underground revolutionary activity that surrounded him in Judah and in Babylon.

Jeremiah delivers instructions from God to the exiles concerning their daily lives and their perspective on their captivity. The exiles are to make a home for themselves in Babylonia. They are to marry, have children, and multiply there, just as the Hebrews did during their slavery in Egypt. The exiles will find their well-being in Babylon's well-being because it is God's will for them to be there. Nebuchadnezzar is God's servant in regard to Israel.

Jeremiah condemns false prophets and magicians among the exiles who lead the people astray (verses 8-9). The exiles face the same conflicting prophecies as do those people left in Jerusalem. Each must discern the true prophetic word and abide by it.

The exiles do make homes for themselves in captivity. They build houses, grow food, and practice their various trades. Babylonian records from this time show payments in oil, barley, and other necessities to foreign captives in exchange for labor, though some captives are used as forced labor. Some Judeans work on construction projects for Nebuchadnezzar. The people are also allowed to assemble and to practice their religion. By 538 B.C., when they are officially allowed to return home, most of the exiles (now in their third generation in Babylon) choose to stay in their new homeland.

The exiles have to reassess their relationship to God. They are away from the Promised Land, from Jerusalem, and from the Temple. They can no longer go to the Temple for worship and sacrifice. Especially after the Temple is destroyed in 587 B.C., they are without that physical symbol and center of God's presence with them. Jeremiah tells them that their faith does not depend on living in the Promised Land nor on Temple sacrifices and ritual (as he does in Jeremiah 7:1-15, 21-22).

The one thing the exiles do have is the Word of God. They can study the holy writings they brought with them. They can listen to and study the words of prophets like Jeremiah, Ezekiel, and Second Isaiah. In the Exile, synagogue-type meetings are held for prayer and teaching. Through all this, the Israelites are on their way to becoming the people of the Word rather than strictly the people of a place (the Promised Land).

Verses 10-14 offer promises for the end of the Exile. God and Israel will then live in a new and mutually fulfilling relationship. Jeremiah assures the exiles that, even without the Temple and its ritual, God will meet them. They can offer themselves to God in their captivity, and God will see to their welfare.

Verses 16-19 break into the order of verses 15 and 20-23. This oracle is directed to those left in Jerusalem rather than to the exiles. It lets the exiles know what is going to happen to their kinsmen. An editor may have put these verses here, using language and images from some of Jeremiah's other prophecies.

Verses 15, 20-23 are a vehement oracle denouncing two prophets living in exile. The Babylonians would execute these men for political subversion rather than for the crimes Jeremiah lists. Jeremiah must communicate more with the exile community than is indicated by the letters of chapter 29, since he knows such details about the private lives and prophecy of these two men.

The Message of Jeremiah 29

Jeremiah's messages to the people of Israel, both in Jerusalem and in exile, are not completely filled with promises of doom. The message in Jeremiah's letter shows that God's plans for Israel go beyond punishment to a more fulfilling future. What are these promises of hope?

§ The exile is not permanent. After seventy years, the people will be able to go home.

§ In the meantime, they can live their normal lives in the confidence that God has not forgotten them.

§ Their new lives after their restoration will be fruitful and happy.

§ God's new covenant with them will bring an inward change and a new knowledge of God.

September 12, 2021

Lesson 2
BEING BOLD TO JOIN

Focal Passage
Luke 7:36-50

Background Text
Mark 2:13-17

Purpose
To grow in sensitivity to the feelings of outsiders, letting that awareness shape our outreach to them

Summary

While God expects those of us who belong to God's people to reach out to others, God also encourages those who do not belong to risk being excluded by joining in without invitation. Luke's story of the woman anointing Jesus' feet makes clear that Jesus will extend an invitation if we take a chance, even when we may feel unworthy or are perceived by others to be unworthy.

SCRIPTURE
Luke 7:36-50

[36]One of the Pharisees invited Jesus to eat with him. After he entered the Pharisee's home, he took his place at the table. [37]Meanwhile, a woman from the city, a sinner, discovered that Jesus was dining in the Pharisee's house. She brought perfumed oil in a vase made of alabaster. [38]Standing behind him at his feet and crying, she began to wet his feet with her tears. She wiped them with her hair, kissed them, and poured the oil on them. [39]When the Pharisee who had invited Jesus saw what was happening, he said to himself, If this man were a prophet, he would know what kind of woman is touching him. He would know that she is a sinner.

[40]Jesus replied, "Simon, I have something to say to you."

"Teacher, speak," he said.

[41]"A certain lender had two debtors. One owed enough money to pay five hundred people for a day's work.[a] The other owed enough money for fifty. [42]When they couldn't pay, the lender forgave the debts of them both. Which of them will love him more?"

[43]Simon replied, "I suppose the one who had the largest debt canceled."

Jesus said, "You have judged correctly."

[44]Jesus turned to the woman and said to Simon, "Do you see this woman? When I entered your home, you didn't give me water for my feet, but she wet my feet with tears and wiped them with her hair. [45]You didn't greet me with a kiss, but she hasn't stopped kissing my feet since I came in. [46]You didn't anoint my head with oil, but she has poured perfumed oil on my feet. [47]This is why I tell you that her many sins have been forgiven; so she has shown great love. The one who is forgiven little loves little."

⁴⁸Then Jesus said to her, "Your sins are forgiven."

⁴⁹The other table guests began to say among themselves, "Who is this person that even forgives sins?"

⁵⁰Jesus said to the woman, "Your faith has saved you. Go in peace."

[a] Luke 7:41 Or *five hundred denaria*

COMMENTARY
Luke 7:36-50

Jesus' ministry moved into ever-widening circles of expression and expectation. More demands were placed upon him; more persons were exposed to him; more reactions took place around him. As he continued his expanding ministry of deed and word, he also began to interpret the nature of the relationship between his gospel and the world of people and powers around him. He both discussed and modeled what it meant to be in the world but not of the world.

Gratitude of the Forgiven

Note that although the *Pharisees* (verse 36) had been critical of him, Jesus still went to dine with them. He took the initiative to bridge gaps. He would not allow their prejudice toward him to prevent his coming to them. His host's name was Simon, the third different person by that name encountered so far in Luke's account (see 4:38; 6:15).

The woman is identified as a *sinner* (verse 37). The original Greek word means "one who has missed the mark." In Jewish usage, it would mean "one who is disobedient to the law and commandments." In using this description of her, Luke expressed the widespread attitude toward her by the people of the area. She was not seen in terms of her name, vocation, family status, or residence—only as a *sinner*.

A Jewish woman often carried a small alabaster container of perfume around her neck. This frequently was one of her most valuable possessions. Her unbound hair would have been a sign of immodesty. The marriage tradition called for a girl to bind up her hair on her wedding day and never again appear in public with it unbound.

It was the custom for persons to remove their sandals upon entering a home. Thus, Jesus would be dining with his feet uncovered. It was also customary for the host to arrange for the washing of the roadway dust from a guest's feet as an expression of hospitality. Anointing the body with olive oil was done after bathing and also used to smooth the hair. It was also offered as an expression of hospitality. For some reason, these had not been arranged by Simon nor had Jesus even been greeted with the usual kiss of welcome (verse 45). So in kissing his feet, using perfume to bathe and anoint them, and wiping them with her hair, this unknown woman of poor reputation expressed both customary courtesy and uncommon devotion.

A *prophet* (verse 39) would have been a person of spiritual understanding and vision, thus knowing the sinful reputation of this person. Her *touching* him in public would have been a mark of shame and the spreading of ceremonial uncleanness.

Denarii (verse 41) were a type of currency. Each denarius would be worth about one-fourth of a cent in present United States currency, but had much more value then.

An interesting new understanding of forgiveness comes in verse 48. Being aware of her own great spiritual need and her own lack of merit, she used this awareness to reach out to others in need, not for merit but out of empathy. Instead of self-despair, she was led to service. For this reason, Jesus described her as *forgiven* (verse 48). In being loved, we find our own needs met. This is the essence of love. But if we have no awareness of need within ourselves, then we may well not have sensitivity to the deep needs of others. Thus, *the one who is forgiven little loves little* (verse 47).

Women also were among the close followers of Jesus, sometimes out of gratitude for his empathy with them and deliverance to them. Mary Magdalene was Mary of Magdalia, a town on the southwest coast of the Sea of Galilee. By some, she is thought to be the woman described earlier in this section who anointed Jesus and was forgiven. There is no proof of this.

The Message of Luke 7:36-50

This section unveils for us a Christ who moves out into the world, motivated and directed by the desire and intention to meet human need. The need may be the need for forgiveness, new insight into truth, a sense of belonging, hope amidst fear, release from the demonic, healing for illness, or life amid death. Human need becomes the magnet for Jesus' ministry. And it is the same for all his disciples, ancient and modern. To believe in Christ is to become his disciple—and to join his mission to witness and to heal!

Lesson 3
OPENING THE DOOR TO CHRIST

Focal Passage
Galatians 2:11-21

Background Tex
Romans 10:1-13

Purpose
To discover how responsible freedom in Christ shapes our lives as Christians in today's world

Summary
Before Jesus Christ, the ritual through which Gentiles entered into God's covenant was circumcision. One had to become a Jew. After Jesus' resurrection, a new path was opened. By entering the covenant of Christ through baptism, one is neither a Jew nor a Gentile. Paul argues against the reestablishment of ritual markers that divide us unnecessarily.

SCRIPTURE
Galatians 2:11-21
[11]But when Cephas came to Antioch, I opposed him to his face, because he was wrong. [12]He had been eating with the Gentiles

before certain people came from James. But when they came, he began to back out and separate himself, because he was afraid of the people who promoted circumcision. [13]And the rest of the Jews also joined him in this hypocrisy so that even Barnabas got carried away with them in their hypocrisy. [14]But when I saw that they weren't acting consistently with the truth of the gospel, I said to Cephas in front of everyone, "If you, though you're a Jew, live like a Gentile and not like a Jew, how can you require the Gentiles to live like Jews?"

[15]We are born Jews—we're not Gentile sinners. [16]However, we know that a person isn't made righteous by the works of the Law but rather through the faithfulness of Jesus Christ. We ourselves believed in Christ Jesus so that we could be made righteous by the faithfulness of Christ and not by the works of the Law—because no one will be made righteous by the works of the Law. [17]But if it is discovered that we ourselves are sinners while we are trying to be made righteous in Christ, then is Christ a servant of sin? Absolutely not! [18]If I rebuild the very things that I tore down, I show that I myself am breaking the Law. [19]I died to the Law through the Law, so that I could live for God. [20]I have been crucified with Christ and I no longer live, but Christ lives in me. And the life that I now live in my body, I live by faith, indeed, by the faithfulness of God's Son, who loved me and gave himself for me. [21]I don't ignore the grace of God, because if we become righteous through the Law, then Christ died for no purpose.

COMMENTARY
Galatians 2:11-21

In this section of Paul's letter to the Galatians, the Jerusalem Conference is still underway (see 2:1). Here, Paul is concerned with ministry to various groups of people, a disagreement with Peter over the relationship between Jews and Gentiles, and the distinction between law and gospel. In the concluding verses of this section, Paul reveals much about his own faith in Jesus Christ.

Paul's Run-in with Peter

The question: Should Jews and Gentiles have table fellowship? Chapter 2:11 indicates that the unity achieved over a handshake in Jerusalem was not always carried out later when it was tested in real circumstances. Christians can often agree to high standards in principle but waver from them in practice. Too often the power of faith is limited by the "buts" in life that cause us to turn aside from the very things we profess to believe the most. In the case Paul discusses in 2:11-21, Peter and James both violated the Jerusalem agreement. Paul says that Peter broke it by being wishy-washy in the faith: He ate first with the Gentiles; but then, seeing the men from James at another table, he changed seats. His motivation, in Paul's view, was fear. He was afraid he would be criticized by the circumcision party for eating anything but kosher food.

The problem, of course, was not just one of food. It was one concerning the fellowship established in 2:9. Paul knew the church could not be one if believers could not even sit down at the same table together. What is more, if they could not eat a meal together, how could they share the Lord's Supper, the clearest symbol of unity in Christ?

It is not clear who those who *came from James* were. Whether or not James, the brother of Jesus, actually approved of their actions is not known. Probably he did, if Paul includes him by name. The fact that they were from James caused Peter to change tables. No doubt he felt safer politically by being with the more powerful men who were from Jerusalem. Peter's action influenced all the other Jews (2:13). And even Barnabas, Paul's traveling companion, insulted the Gentiles by moving. Paul's language about these activities is very descriptive.

Drew back (verse 12 NRSV; *back out*, CEB) is a military and political term which defines a retreat to a safer position. He puts it in the

Greek imperfect tense to indicate that this was not an isolated incident, but something Peter customarily did. Paul's words literally mean *he kept on drawing back*. It reminds us of the word *deserting* in 1:6.

Hypocrisy (verse 13), in its most basic sense, means "pretense, play-acting." Peter and the others were acting; they were insincere when they first sat down with the Gentiles. Jesus repeatedly applies the same word to the hypocrisy of the Pharisees (Matthew 23:28; Mark 12:15; Luke 12:1; also see Matthew 23:13-15, 23-29; Mark 7:6; Luke 6:42).

Paul knows Peter and the men from James are wrong in their actions in Antioch because such behavior denies the essential oneness of all Christians in Christ. Christians are united because Christ is one and because they are all saved from sin in the same way. Christ did not die on the cross so the Jews could be saved by one method and the Gentiles by another. All people, whether Jews or Gentiles, are put right only by God's free gift in Christ; they are only justified by faith. In 2:14-21, Paul introduces his important concept of justification by faith alone, one which he expands in Galatians 3–4 and develops most fully in Romans 1:18–4:25. As he says in Romans 3:23-24, "All have sinned and fall short of God's glory, but all are treated as righteous freely by his grace."

Throughout Galatians 2:14-21 and in the rest of the letter, the words *justify* and *justification* are very important. In its most basic sense, *justification* refers to the taking away of guilt and making a person innocent. In English, it is often translated "being put right" with God. Justification has a legal sense about it, indicating that someone must do something to remove guilt and create a not-guilty verdict. Paul argues in Romans that the normal sentence for human sin is the death penalty (Romans 6:23; see Genesis 3:19). The Jews believed that by observing the rules of the law (Galatians 2:16, 19; see the discussion in reference to 1:14), they could earn salvation. Paul denies such a thing is possible. Being put right with God is only possible through faith in Jesus Christ (2:16). People cannot do anything to be put right with God, but they can believe

15

in the power of God's action in Christ, that is, the raising of Jesus from the dead. They can believe he is the Son of God (Romans 10:9).

Then, and only then, will they be justified. *Faith* (2:16) means trust in God, who is trustworthy in every way. Paul says we cannot get salvation the old-fashioned way—we cannot earn it.

Turning from Paul's concept of justification to the structure of Galatians 2:11-21 as a whole, it must be admitted that it is difficult to know just how the verses have been organized by him. Bible scholars are not certain where Paul's reprimand of Peter ends and his comments to the Galatians begin again. In verse 17, Paul poses a rhetorical question. Possibly some of the men from James may have put it to him to discredit his arguments. The question is: If we are put right with God through faith and are still found to be sinning anyway, do we not then make Christ an agent or a servant of sin? In other words, by falling back into sin, are we not making Christ's death on the cross useless and actually forcing him to encourage sin? Paul's answer is a forceful *absolutely not* (CEB; *certainly not!* NRSV) This is a favorite expression of Paul's. Literally, it can be translated "God forbid, be it not so, by no means, nothing doing, or no way." He uses it frequently in his writings to refute arguments against the truth of his gospel (Romans 3:3-6, 31; 6:2, 15; 7:7, 13; 9:14; 1 Corinthians 6:15; Galatians 3:21). The fact that Christians are still sinners does not nullify (Galatians 2:21) the grace of God. Justification is not determined by observance of the law—what the believer does not or does do. It is determined by what Christ did and what the believer believes.

In Galatians 2:19-20, Paul turns to some personal expressions of the meaning of faith that will help his readers understand their own relationship to Christ. These verses contain some of the most lyrical and beautiful words that Paul ever wrote and they, along with 1 Corinthians 13, have inspired Christians for centuries with their depth of feeling. Key expressions in these verses are *with Christ* and *in Christ*. Paul says that he is crucified with Christ; Christ lives in him; he lives by faith in the Son of God. These propositions of faith indicate how close Paul was to Jesus and why he knew that his gospel was true. Paul implies that the believer should be so close to Christ that Christ is part of the atmosphere that is breathed and inhaled. To use a modern example, it could be said that being in Christ is like a cup of hot tea. Christ is infused into the Christian like a teabag placed in a cup of hot water. Whether the teabag is in the water or the water is in the teabag is impossible to tell. Eventually, the tea and the water are all the same as the tea flows into the water and the water goes through the teabag. Thus, Paul can say that Christ is in him or that he is in Christ; it does not really matter. The image shows how much he feels the love of Christ in him and how much it influences every thought and action. (For other places where Paul builds on the idea of being *in Christ*, see Romans 3:24; 6:11, 23; 1 Corinthians 1:4; 2 Corinthians 2:17.)

Paul's words in verse 19 mean that law is removed as a powerful force in his life, that it no longer has any control over him or claim upon him. To *live for God* (CEB; *to God,* NRSV) is Paul's expression for true living, the very essence of life and the way a Christian acts on a day-to-day basis (Galatians 5:25; Romans 6:8). Indeed, in a famous passage in Philippians 1:21, Paul shows that the meaning of life for him is entirely wrapped up in Jesus Christ when he says, "Because for me, living serves Christ."

The Message of Galatians 2:7-21

§ Paul is entrusted with the gospel, to interpret it as best he can and to preach it to his audience.

§ Genuine disagreements and differences in interpretation of law and tradition characterized the early church, just as they characterize today's church.

§ Faith in Jesus Christ is essential if one is to be justified (in right relationship with God).

September 26, 2021

Lesson 4
CITIZENS OF GOD'S HOUSEHOLD

Focal Passages
Ephesians 2:19-22

Background Text
Philippians 3:2-21; Ephesians 2:11-22

Purpose
To discover the privileges and responsibilities of being a citizen in God's household

Summary
In the ancient world, citizenship was limited to an elite group of people, and the benefits and protection of the city were limited to its citizens. Individuals and communities actively sought Roman citizenship as a sign of their status and a means to lucrative rewards. The early church offered citizenship to everyone in a context in which they were minorities in a community/society that greeted them with hostility. This divinely granted honor is based not upon the quest for glory and material wealth—these, Paul counts as rubbish—but upon conforming to the self-sacrificial life of Christ.

SCRIPTURE
Philippians 3:2-21

²Watch out for the "dogs." Watch out for people who do evil things. Watch out for those who insist on circumcision, which is really mutilation. ³We are the circumcision. We are the ones who serve by God's Spirit and who boast in Christ Jesus. We don't put our confidence in rituals performed on the body, ⁴though I have good reason to have this kind of confidence. If anyone else has reason to put their confidence in physical advantages, I have even more:

⁵I was circumcised on the eighth day.
I am from the people of Israel and the tribe of Benjamin.
I am a Hebrew of the Hebrews.
With respect to observing the Law, I'm a Pharisee.
⁶With respect to devotion to the faith, I harassed the church.
With respect to righteousness under the Law, I'm blameless.

⁷These things were my assets, but I wrote them off as a loss for the sake of Christ. ⁸But even beyond that, I consider everything a loss in comparison with the superior value of knowing Christ Jesus my Lord. I have lost everything for him, but what I lost I think of as sewer trash, so that I might gain Christ ⁹and be found in him. In Christ I have a righteousness that is not my own and that does not come from the Law but rather from the faithfulness of Christ. It is the righteousness of God that is based on faith. ¹⁰The righteousness that I have comes from knowing Christ, the power of his resurrection, and the participation in his sufferings. It includes being conformed to his death ¹¹so that I may perhaps reach the goal of the resurrection of the dead.

¹²It's not that I have already reached this goal or have already been perfected, but I pursue it, so that I may grab hold of it because Christ grabbed hold of me for just this purpose. ¹³Brothers and sisters, I myself don't think I've reached it, but I do this one thing: I forget about the things behind

me and reach out for the things ahead of me. [14]The goal I pursue is the prize of God's upward call in Christ Jesus. [15]So all of us who are spiritually mature should think this way, and if anyone thinks differently, God will reveal it to him or her. [16]Only let's live in a way that is consistent with whatever level we have reached.

[17]Brothers and sisters, become imitators of me and watch those who live this way—you can use us as models. [18]As I have told you many times and now say with deep sadness, many people live as enemies of the cross. [19]Their lives end with destruction. Their god is their stomach, and they take pride in their disgrace because their thoughts focus on earthly things. [20]Our citizenship is in heaven.

We look forward to a savior that comes from there—the Lord Jesus Christ. [21]He will transform our humble bodies so that they are like his glorious body, by the power that also makes him able to subject all things to himself.

Ephesians 2:19-22

[19]So now you are no longer strangers and aliens. Rather, you are fellow citizens with God's people, and you belong to God's household. [20]As God's household, you are built on the foundation of the apostles and prophets with Christ Jesus himself as the cornerstone. [21]The whole building is joined together in him, and it grows up into a temple that is dedicated to the Lord. [22]Christ is building you into a place where God lives through the Spirit.

COMMENTARY
Philippians 3:2-21

One major threat to the church is yet to be considered: false teaching about the way of salvation, advocated by *enemies of the cross* of Christ (3:18). If their way to righteousness (salvation) is wrong, what is the true way, as Paul conceives it? The whole of chapter 3 deals with this question.

Renunciation of Assets (3:2-8)

Paul's assets, utterly renounced as giving him credit before God, were (1) assets from national background and heredity, and (2) assets from personal choice and achievement.

In the first group are: proper Jewish childhood circumcision (on the eighth day), privileged national and tribal origin (from the divinely chosen people of Israel and the esteemed tribe of Benjamin), pure Hebrew blood, and upbringing in untainted Hebrew culture (the Greek text reads "a Hebrew of Hebrews").

In the second group are: membership in the Pharisaic party (a party honored for conscientious and detailed obedience to the Mosaic law), zealous activity in that sect in upholding the law (by persecution of lawless Christians), and faultless personal performance of the law's requirements for right living.

These striking assets led Paul to put *confidence in the flesh,* that is, in his human privileges and achievements. Such confidence gave him a righteousness (rightness) of his own making (verse 9), a self-righteousness (Romans 10:1-3). It did not put him in right relationship with God. Such a relationship cannot come by human performance of the commands of the law, he says, however good that performance may be.

In fact, as he points out in Romans and Galatians, the more one studies the law and seeks to become righteous by it, the more one comes under the power of the sin that operates through it and becomes subject to the death that sin brings (Romans 7:5, 10-11). The law promotes sin by negative stimulation: by making a person want to do what the law forbids. The law's only function is to make sin recognizable (Romans 3:20; 5:13; 7:7) and to point to the Savior (Galatians 3:22-24), who alone has power to defeat sin and put one in right relationship with God. Thus, human assets and human effort are worthless.

Faith-Identification with Christ (3:9-11)

Human assets, as a ground of acceptance with God, must be jettisoned if one is to come to *know* Christ. For Paul and the biblical writers in general, to know God or Christ involves much more than to have knowledge *about* God or Christ. It means to be in intimate, humble, adoring, and obedient relation to them. Personal, experiential knowledge is meant here.

According to the present passage, to *know* Christ means to be *found in him* and thus, to have his righteousness (the rightness he has before God) at the day of judgment. It also means to experience the power he wields by virtue of his resurrection, to share his sufferings (both in his death on the cross and in the sufferings of the church as his body), and to have the blessed hope of ultimate resurrection from the dead (meaning, from among the physically dead). Present Christian experience, while a foretaste of the final life in the kingdom of God, is not the full realization of redemption, as the false teachers held.

Faith in Christ (verse 9) is complete surrender to and personal trust in Christ, not trust in one's assets and achievements. It is the response of the whole self to the God who is presented in Jesus Christ.

Progressing in Christ (3:12-16)

The false teachers seem to have believed that they became perfect at the time of their baptismal birth in Christ. They maintained they were enjoying now the fullness of the life of the kingdom of God. Nothing more was to be expected. Paul refutes this vehemently.

Knowing Christ is an ongoing experience, he says. Perfect life in Christ is not achievable in this life, but only at the transformation to be experienced at the coming of Christ (3:20-21). Paul continues to speak in the first person, using himself as an example of what he means. Like a runner in a race, I forget what lies behind me (my assets from heredity and achievements, my sins and failures, and my attainments as a

Christian) and continually press on, *straining* to reach the goal-marker and to obtain the prize at the end of the race.

What the prize is, Paul does not say. Is the prize God's call to come up and inherit the Kingdom? Is the prize full knowledge of Christ, of which Paul has had a growing but incomplete experience? Is it resurrection life (verse 11) with Christ? Probably all of these. Second Corinthians 5:1-10 shows the prize to be an eternal new order of incomparable glory, made by God and not by human hands, where we shall be clothed with a new body and be *at home with the Lord* (2 Corinthians 5:8).

Following Models (3:17-21)

Paul knows teaching is not enough. Truth must be embodied in life if it is to have compelling power. In chapter 2, he gave the Philippians teaching (2:1-4). And then he offered them models to follow: Christ and Timothy and Epaphroditus.

The Philippians can be helped on in the true way of salvation if they pay attention to heaven-oriented, not earth-minded, leaders: Paul and those whose lives are patterned after his. Earth-minded leaders will lead them into libertine indulgence and final destruction.

We should not set our minds on earthly things, Paul says, because our *citizenship* (homeland) is in heaven. Our life while here should be in keeping with what we are and with our destiny. That destiny will be realized when our Savior, the Lord Jesus Christ, will come from heaven to transform our bodies (that is, our persons) by his unlimited power into his own glorious likeness.

The Message of Philippians 3

§ Assets from heredity and personal achievements, if trusted in for salvation, are a hindrance to God's favor and blessings. Salvation is by faith alone. The bringer of that salvation is Jesus Christ, who *gave himself for our sins, so he could deliver us from this present evil age* (Galatians 1:4). *A person isn't made righteous by the works of the Law but rather through the faithfulness of Jesus Christ* (Galatians 2:16). *Self-righteousness* comes through human assets and works, but not God's righteousness (that is, a right relationship with God).

§ If this is so, then all modern religions of achievement must be ineffective. This includes those forms of Protestantism that stress salvation through education and becoming through doing.

§ Also important is Paul's position that being *in Christ* during this life brings with it no absolute perfection. We *press on* in the knowledge that that goal is yet to be reached. We are Christians in the making, ever seeking to become actually that which we became ideally at the point of beginning.

Ephesians 2:19-22

In this section, the author of Ephesians demonstrates how the ancient distinction between Jews and Gentiles has been demolished by Christ.

You Are Now Fellow Citizens (2:19)

At one time, the distinction was drawn so severely between Jews and Gentiles that the Gentiles must have felt as though they were aliens and refugees in the city of God. Although the Jews were commanded to treat strangers and sojourners with special care (Deuteronomy 10:18-19; 27:19; Job 31:32), outsiders were governed by different laws (Leviticus 24:22) and were probably generally regarded with suspicion. In Greek and Roman cities, citizenship was usually dependent on birth rather than residence, and a foreigner could gain it only by special decree. Citizenship was a very valuable commodity in the Roman Empire and, without it, one might not have equal protection under the law (see Acts 22:22-29). In Ephesians 2:19, the writer makes it clear that such distinctions do not exist in the church of Jesus Christ. The Gentiles are now citizens with the saints (those set apart or called by God to be in the church, 1:1) and members of the household of God.

The household rules in Ephesians 5:21–6:9 are a variation of the kind of expectations that most people understood. In Roman society, for example, people were connected through these codes, not so much by feelings of love as by hierarchical order. Individuals were to obey the emperor, the nation, and the head of the house (usually the father), in that order (see Romans 13:1; 1 Peter 2:13-14, 17). In some circles, it was believed that if order in the family could be preserved, then all larger institutions could be expected to survive. If a father could not control his own house, on the other hand, how could he, or anyone else, be expected to govern a city or a nation (or a church: see 1 Timothy 3:4-5)? The author of Ephesians builds on this kind of understanding when he tells Christians their household is built on a somewhat different order. Christians do not owe primary honor to the emperor, but to Jesus Christ. He is the head of their house (1:22; 5:22-24), and Gentiles and Jews both are children in it.

The Foundation and Cornerstone (2:20)

The writer continues with the metaphor of the house and the church. The church of Jesus Christ is God's new house *built upon the foundation of the apostles and prophets*. This verse is an indication that Ephesians probably was not written by the apostle Paul. The writer indicates here that Jesus is the keystone of the church (as *cornerstone* should correctly be translated), but the apostles and prophets (Christian prophets; see 1 Corinthians 12:10) are the *foundation*. The apostle Paul, however, thinks of Jesus Christ alone as the foundation and cornerstone in 1 Corinthians 3:11. It is extremely unlikely, furthermore, that he would refer to the apostles as the building blocks of the church as if he were not among them himself. As he demonstrates repeatedly in Galatians, his apostleship is a critical part of the proof of his authority.

25

The image of Jesus as the cornerstone of the church is a common one in the New Testament (Matthew 21:42; Acts 4:11; 1 Peter 2:4-8), and Ephesians reflects a time in the life of the church when Christians were trying to determine who should have power in the church. The author indicates here that leaders have to be in line with the original founders of the church who had the titles of prophets and apostles.

The Living House (2:21-22)

Verses 21-22 complete the comparison of the house and the church by picturing the church as a building that is a living being, an organism in which God lives. Here, he builds on the Old Testament idea that the place in which God is worshipped is the house in which God dwells (2 Chronicles 5:14; Psalm 122:1). He also uses a physiological model: The house of God is like a human body, intricately put together with tissue, bones, and joints (see 4:15-16). For him, the church is no longer a dwelling place, a building, or a steeple. The church is a living body; it is people (see 1 Peter 2:5; 4:17).

The Message of Ephesians 2:11-22

§ Gentiles also are no longer alienated from God as they were at one time. They are not aliens and refugees in God's city anymore, but are now full citizens with equal rights and privileges.

§ Jesus Christ has broken down the wall between Jews and Gentiles which was symbolized by the wall that kept Gentiles out of the Jerusalem Temple. He has broken down the fence which the law put around the Jews. He has destroyed the hostility that existed between God and humanity. Through his blood, his sacrifice on the cross, Christ has brought peace.

§ Gentiles now coexist as members of one family, brothers and sisters in one household of God. Together, they make up a living house which is where God may dwell and truly be worshipped.

UNIT 2
October 2021

INTO THE FUTURE

Introduction to the Unit

After over two thousand years of existence as an institution, we can easily take for granted that we know what the church is. This unit invites readers to look at it from the view of the community living into the future. The Greek word for church, *ekklesia,* is not a word that the first members of the church associated with a religious activity. The word signifies the assembly of the people of God. It is instructive to look at what their understanding of the purpose of assembling as a group signified, how it has shaped our understanding of church, and how reading these texts might renew and expand our understanding.

October 3, 2021

Lesson 5
THE CHURCH'S ACTIVITIES

Focal Passage
Acts 2:37-47

Background Text
Acts 2:37-47; 4:32-37

Purpose
To discover how the early church was shaped by the Holy Spirit and
how the Holy Spirit still shapes the church today

Summary
The church is inaugurated by the coming of the Holy Spirit at
Pentecost (Acts 2:1-4). Acts 2:37-47 provides an overview of the many
activities in which the assembled group of new believers engaged
spontaneously. After two thousand years, what have we let fall by the
wayside? What practices have we retained but regulated in such a way
that they have lost their Pentecost energy? What do we continue to do
that makes assembling meaningful?

SCRIPTURE
Acts 2:37-47

37When the crowd heard this, they were deeply troubled. They said to Peter and the other apostles, "Brothers, what should we do?"

38Peter replied, "Change your hearts and lives. Each of you must be baptized in the name of Jesus Christ for the forgiveness of your sins. Then you will receive the gift of the Holy Spirit. 39This promise is for you, your children, and for all who are far away—as many as the Lord our God invites." 40With many other words he testified to them and encouraged them, saying, "Be saved from this perverse generation." 41Those who accepted Peter's message were baptized. God brought about three thousand people into the community on that day.

42The believers devoted themselves to the apostles' teaching, to the community, to their shared meals, and to their prayers. 43A sense of awe came over everyone. God performed many wonders and signs through the apostles. 44All the believers were united and shared everything. 45They would sell pieces of property and possessions and distribute the proceeds to everyone who needed them. 46Every day, they met together in the temple and ate in their homes. They shared food with gladness and simplicity. 47They praised God and demonstrated God's goodness to everyone. The Lord added daily to the community those who were being saved.

COMMENTARY
Acts 2:37-47

The first two chapters of Acts introduce the reader to both a remarkable document and a series of events. The book itself is a continuation of the work of Jesus. No other such book survives. We have no other record. The history to which it gives witness is that of the apostolic age. Three major events form the content of these chapters: the risen Christ (the Resurrection), Christ's ascension, and finally the unprecedented phenomenon of Pentecost.

Throughout the Book of Acts, the presence and work of the Holy Spirit are primary concerns. However, Luke also attempts to present a complete or systematic theology of the Spirit. The narrative of how the Christian message spreads quickens the imagination as the expansion of Christianity has to work through internal as well as external resistance.

The first part of chapter 2 of Acts shares the story of Pentecost and Peter's sermon. The term used for early Christian preaching is *kerygma*. Peter's sermon contains many of the essential elements of the kerygma:

1. prophecies in Scripture fulfilled (2:17-21)
2. Jesus born of the seed of David (2:25)
3. Jesus died to deliver us, according to Scripture
4. Jesus was buried
5. Jesus rose
6. Jesus is exalted at the right hand of God (2:33)
7. Jesus will come again.

Response to the Preached Word (2:37-42)

An appropriate response to preaching is repentance. Baptism is not necessarily required for the promise of the Holy Spirit. That is, an outward sign or action is not required.

Four disciplines characterize the early Christians: (1) instruction by the apostles, (2) contribution of offering, (3) communal meals, and (4) prayers.

The Christian movement is one of great vigor and vitality among Jews who continue to be a part of their Temple. Thus far, Christians have evoked little resistance.

A Description of the Early Church (2:43-47)

Luke summarizes through vivid and concise images and scenes what would otherwise require a great deal more time and space. Other similar summaries will occur later on in the Book of Acts (4:32-35; 5:12-15). The new Christian community centers on a shared common life that is celebrated regularly. Evidently, the power of this way of living attracts thousands of converts within a very short time.

The Message of Acts 2

The first two chapters of Acts recount remarkable events and truths. The power and truth is not restricted to a single historical era. We must ask what the significance of these events is for our generation as well as for the early church. What, then, do these chapters tell us about God and God's work with us?

§ Election is by God.

§ The task of Christianity is not to passively await Christ's return. Rather, Christians must establish new relationships to the world in which they live.

§ The real boundaries are never geographical; they are religious, national, and racial.

§ The Holy Spirit sometimes breaks up comfortable and familiar patterns.

§ God's summons is both filled with promise and laden with responsibility.

§ God's power exceeds even the power of death.

§ Christ will return.

§ The Holy Spirit is available to all.

§ The Christian community is characterized by its care, discipline, and prayer.

Lesson 6
THE CHURCH AS ONE BODY

Focal Passage
1 Corinthians 12:12-31

Background Text
1 Corinthians 12:1-31

Purpose
To let Paul guide us in celebrating and sharing the unique gifts God has given each of us in building up Christ's body

Summary
Being an assembled body transformed individuals into one shared identity in which the whole became greater than the parts. Paul emphasizes the need to share our gifts with each other, not just as a virtue. The gifts are a divine gift given for a particular purpose. They are the means by which the community is constituted and enact God's ministry.

SCRIPTURE
1 Corinthians 12:12-31

[12]Christ is just like the human body—a body is a unit and has many parts; and all the parts of the body are one body, even though there are many. [13]We were all baptized by one Spirit into one body, whether Jew or Greek, or slave or free, and we all were given one Spirit to drink. [14]Certainly the body isn't one part but many. [15]If the foot says, "I'm not part of the body because I'm not a hand," does that mean it's not part of the body? [16]If the ear says, "I'm not part of the body because I'm not an eye," does that mean it's not part of the body? [17]If the whole body were an eye, what would happen to the hearing? And if the whole body were an ear, what would happen to the sense of smell? [18]But as it is, God has placed each one of the parts in the body just like he wanted. [19]If all were one and the same body part, what would happen to the body? [20]But as it is, there are many parts but one body. [21]So the eye can't say to the hand, "I don't need you," or in turn, the head can't say to the feet, "I don't need you." [22]Instead, the parts of the body that people think are the weakest are the most necessary. [23]The parts of the body that we think are less honorable are the ones we honor the most. The private parts of our body that aren't presentable are the ones that are given the most dignity. [24]The parts of our body that are presentable don't need this. But God has put the body together, giving greater honor to the part with less honor [25]so that there won't be division in the body and so the parts might have mutual concern for each other. [26]If one part suffers, all the parts suffer with it; if one part gets the glory, all the parts celebrate with it. [27]You are the body of Christ and parts of each other. [28]In the church, God has appointed first apostles, second prophets, third teachers, then miracles, then gifts of healing, the ability to help others, leadership skills, different kinds of tongues. [29]All aren't apostles,

are they? All aren't prophets, are they? All aren't teachers, are they? All don't perform miracles, do they? [30]All don't have gifts of healing, do they? All don't speak in different tongues, do they? All don't interpret, do they? [31]Use your ambition to try to get the greater gifts. And I'm going to show you an even better way.

COMMENTARY

1 Corinthians 12:12-31

The central activity of the believers at Corinth was worship. Chapter 12 focuses mainly on the place of spiritual gifts within the worshipping community.

Comments About Spiritual Gifts (12:1-31)

How are *spiritual gifts* or spiritual persons to be understood? Paul does not want the Corinthians to be uninformed about this matter. Some Corinthian believers had worshipped idols, proving that their apparent spirituality was exclusively self-motivated. But be assured that Christian spirituality does not come from self or any other source. Because the Spirit of God comes through Christ, no believer could ever say, "Jesus is cursed!" (verse 3). But the opposite is also true. No unbeliever could ever say, "Jesus is the Lord," without the guidance of the Holy Spirit. Paul's test of spirituality is clear: Everything comes from God and returns to God through Christ in the Spirit.

All the different gifts of God come through the same Holy Spirit. The source is the same; the gifts must be seen from God's perspective, not the perspective of humanity. These gifts indicate types of service in the Lord. So, gifts and service are bound together, just as the Holy Spirit and Christ are bound together. And as Christ and the Spirit are God's message to humanity, so a believer's gifts and service enable a Christian to live out a thankful response to God. For Paul, the threefold God (Trinity) means a threefold experience in the life of the believer. This threefold response of gift, service, and thanksgiving is given for one purpose: that of upbuilding the community of faith.

From the source of the Spirit come diverse gifts: *a word* (CEB; *utterance,* NRSV) *of wisdom* and *knowledge* (verse 8), referring to practical discourses, teaching, and counseling; gifts of *faith,* or strong members witnessing to the source of the community; *healing,* both spiritual and physical; gifts of the *performance of miracles, prophecy,* spiritual discernment, various kinds of *tongues,* and *interpretation of tongues* (verse 10). These gifts are apparently known by the Corinthian believers. The one Spirit of God gives these gifts, not in accordance with humanity's desires but in accordance with God's will and for the health of the community.

Why does the Spirit give diverse gifts? Paul uses the analogy of the body to explain how the Spirit comes from God and gives gifts to persons in accordance with God's will (not humanity's). A body is unified, but has several parts. The many individuals of the body of Christ are not only unified in Christ but receive from Christ, through the Spirit, an assigned gift and place of service. The Spirit comes from God. Believers baptized into one body drink the same Spirit. This is the unity and diversity of Corinth's house churches.

Paul pushes this analogy further. The nature of a body is a unity of many parts. On the one hand, one part cannot justly say that because it is not some other part of the body, it does not belong. Perhaps some house church members in Corinth were arguing and competing over certain tasks and responsibilities within the community. On the other hand, everyone cannot be one part of the body. This would deny the very nature of body. Rather, the body is naturally created and ordered by God.

So it is with the church, the body of Christ. The many are in the one. Parts of the body do not have the natural or spiritual right to discharge or cut off any other part of the body. The parts of the body that have the hidden and most discreet gifts have, in fact, the most important gifts. It is not the most visible gifts that are of the greatest importance to the community, such as speaking in tongues. The showiness of certain gifts indicates that they are the least important. Perhaps Paul is remembering certain individuals who had promoted such thinking among the house churches in Corinth. Paul is quite clear that the lesser gifts receive greater honor in the assemblies and the unpresentable parts are treated with greater modesty (verses 23-24).

God's creation of the body has a beautiful naturalness. The weaker and humbler parts are, in fact, the stronger because, as with Paul, God is made strong in weakness (2 Corinthians 12:10). This naturalness keeps strife from entering the body. There is no competing or struggling in the body because each part knows its gifts, its place of service, and its means of thankful response to God. The elimination of competition allows for an environment of caring, concern, and upbuilding. What happens to one happens to all—good or bad.

What does all this mean? Paul explains what he has been trying to say in a summary paragraph (verses 27-31). The Corinthian believers are *the body of Christ* collectively and individually (verse 27). Paul now lists God-ordained assignments in order of importance (see Ephesians 4:11-16): apostles (or preachers), prophets (also proclaimers of the gospel), teachers, miracle workers, healers, helpers, administrators, and those who speak in tongues. Then Paul asks if all could do one task or if all should be the same. Of course not! They should struggle and seek the *greater gifts*, or the gifts that have less showiness. According to Paul's ordering, at least some Corinthians sought the lowest gift of all, that of speaking in tongues. Value those higher gifts on my list, says Paul. From this discussion, Paul launches into a profound statement about the gift of God to humanity. God's gift exceeds all gifts of the Spirit. God's gift is the gift of love. The gift of God is *a still more excellent way* (NRSV) or an even better way (CEB).

These two chapters conclude the narrative part of Matthew's section four on the church. Through the events that happen here, Jesus teaches his disciples what it will mean to be an apostle and to minister in the church. They are with him in controversy with the Pharisees and Sadducees learning to beware of the corrupting leaven of their teaching. After Peter's confession, Jesus tells his disciples he will suffer many things from the elders and chief priests and will be killed. When Peter protests this announcement, Jesus rebukes him as a man who speaks for Satan. The disciples are told that they, too, must take up the same cross as Jesus. In discovering that they cannot heal an epileptic boy, the disciples learn that healing requires more than a little faith. Finally, Jesus teaches the need to compromise sometimes in order not to give offense. We can say in all truth that this section represents "field education" for the disciples.

Peter's Confession of Faith (16:13-28)

The remaining sixteen verses of this chapter have a unity of purpose easily overlooked as we consider closely each of the four parts: verses 13-16, 17-20, 21-23, and 24-28. Matthew has used the original account of the event as it appears in Mark 8:27–9:1. But he has added material to serve the later purpose of his Gospel. Some of his additions reflect more of a post-Resurrection faith than what might have been said at the time. We will first sketch the overall intention of Matthew's design, and then consider some details of his account.

Matthew wants it understood that Jesus is the Christ, the chosen one of God. He is the one for whom all others were forerunners, especially Elijah and John the Baptist (verses 14-16). Such a claim is made on the basis not of logic but of a direct revelation from God (verse 17). It must be clear, however, that Jesus fits no traditional expectation of the Messiah; he will suffer at the hands of the elders and chief priests and be killed. However, he will be raised by God from the dead (verse 21).

Because of these things, the followers of Jesus will make their life together in the church bearing the name of Jesus (verse 18). To Peter will be given authority to make both temporal and eternal judgments (verse 19). These things will come to pass, even before all the disciples have died (verse 28).

Such a scenario clearly fits the situation for which Matthew prepared his Gospel. We may consider it unlikely that Jesus foresaw a "Christian" church, bearing his name and separated from Israel. But by the time Matthew wrote, that separation was taking place. The new wine of the gospel had burst the old wineskins of the institutions of Israel. Even if Jesus did recognize himself as God's Messiah, he wanted no such announcement to be made. People would not only misunderstand the kind of messiah Jesus asserted himself to be, but the opposition would have silenced him immediately. Instead, he commanded secrecy from the disciples, and warned them and all who came after them that they, too, would suffer, even as he had.

Caesarea Philippi was a pagan city named by Herod's son, Philip, in honor of one of the caesars and of himself. It was located among the fertile sources of the Jordan River on the southwestern slope of Mount Hermon. It is ironic that this city, where tradition places Peter's definitive confession of Christian faith, was the site of an ancient shrine to Pan, the Greek god of fertility and flocks.

Matthew adds to the original account the *Son of the living God* (verse 16) in order to make clear that Jesus is more than a divinely-anointed king of Israel, which is what the term *Christ* meant in Jewish messianic hope.

Only in Matthew do we read of Jesus' response to Peter's confession. No other words of Jesus have provoked such partisan debate as these! Upon them, the Roman Catholic Church has based its structure of the ecclesiastical hierarchy deriving from the "primacy of Peter." Most non-Roman scholars understand these words to indicate Peter as the first witness of the Resurrection and, therefore, as the prime apostolic witness that God raised Jesus from the dead.

Away from me, Satan! recalls the temptation of Jesus (4:10 NIV). Here Peter speaks for Satan in trying to distract Jesus from the way of the cross.

We note that Jesus speaks of the Son of Man in the third person: *the Son of Man is to come* (NRSV; *human one*, CEB). Possibly, Jesus did not identify himself with the apocalyptic judge of the end time. Whatever title he may have used to identify himself, Jesus believed he had a vocation from God unlike that of any other person.

The Message of Matthew 16

"Who do you say that I am?" Jesus asked Peter. Supposedly, you know me best. Who am I? Matthew, through his Gospel, sends Jesus' question down the corridors of history to our time and place. Who do *we* say Jesus is? As far as our lives are concerned, this is the ultimate question. It does make a difference whether we say Jesus is one whom we can trust with our sin when we need forgiveness, whose light we can follow in darkness, in whose word we can find comfort when life tumbles in. Blessed are we when we can say, "Jesus is the Christ, Son of the living God!"

What are we putting on the scale to "balance" God's gift of life? Acquisitions; popularity; insulation from the world's pain; the cries of the hungry, the lonely, the desperate; insurance that we will never lose our life for anyone or anything but ourselves? Or are we willing to give up these things if only we could be given back our souls, our freedom to love God and neighbors?

There can be no healing, whether of physical, moral, emotional, or spiritual distress, without faith. Faith alone may not move a mountain to yonder place. But without faith in a power that gives life, nothing will move.

Lesson 8
THE NEED FOR SPIRITUAL RENEWAL

Focal Passage
Revelation 3:1-6, 14-20

Background Text
Romans 12:9-17

Purpose
To become aware of the signs and causes of spiritual stagnation, and develop a coping strategy

Summary
John compares the works of the churches in Sardis to that of dead people, and in Laodicea to the lukewarm water that one spits out. He urges them to approach their work with earnestness. One of the challenges of becoming an assembly of people, unlike political parties or clubs, is to continue to find ways of renewing the passion that originally brought us together.

SCRIPTURE
Revelation 3:1-6

"Write this to the angel of the church in Sardis:

These are the words of the one who holds God's seven spirits and the seven stars: I know your works. You have the reputation of being alive, and you are in fact dead. ²Wake up and strengthen whatever you have left, teetering on the brink of death, for I've found that your works are far from complete in the eyes of my God. ³So remember what you received and heard. Hold on to it and change your hearts and lives. If you don't wake up, I will come

like a thief, and you won't know what time I will come upon you. ⁴But you do have a few people in Sardis who haven't stained their clothing. They will walk with me clothed in white because they are worthy. ⁵Those who emerge victorious will wear white clothing like this. I won't scratch out their names from the scroll of life, but will declare their names in the presence of my Father and his angels. ⁶If you can hear, listen to what the Spirit is saying to the churches."

Revelation 3:14-20

¹⁴"Write this to the angel of the church in Laodicea:

These are the words of the Amen, the faithful and true witness, the ruler[a] of God's creation. ¹⁵I know your works. You are neither cold nor hot. I wish that you were either cold or hot. ¹⁶So because you are lukewarm, and neither hot nor cold, I'm about to spit you out of

my mouth. ¹⁷After all, you say, 'I'm rich, and I've grown wealthy, and I don't need a thing.' You don't realize that you are miserable, pathetic, poor, blind, and naked. ¹⁸My advice is that you buy gold from me that has been purified by fire so that you may be rich, and white clothing to wear so that your nakedness won't be shamefully exposed, and ointment to put on your eyes so that you may see. [19]I correct and discipline those whom I love. So be earnest and change your hearts and lives. [20]Look! I'm standing at the door and knocking. If any hear my voice and open the door, I will come in to be with them, and will have dinner with them, and they will have dinner with me."

---

[a] Revelation 3:14 Or *beginning*

COMMENTARY
Revelation 3:1-22

There were more than seven churches in Asia Minor. The number seven had symbolic significance, meaning *all*, *complete*, or *perfect*. The seven churches were important in themselves, but they also stand for all of the church. What afflicted them afflicted the entire church. What was promised them was promised the entire church.

The order of the letters to the seven churches is no accident. Ephesus, the first mentioned, lies closest to the island of Patmos. Smyrna, the next, rests to the north. From there on, the route connecting these large cities of Asia Minor forms a loop—roughly, the very path one would take traveling on foot to deliver mail. Clearly, John knew the main travel arteries of the area. He knew the cities and their churches as well. Each letter he writes speaks directly to the condition of the church and to the mischief caused by its environment.

The inland churches (Thyatira, Sardis, Philadelphia, and Laodicea) were not spared either strife or temptation. Three of the four had yielded.

Sardis erred because it forgot what it had been taught. Its beliefs forgotten, its works wandered down dangerous pathways. In truth, this hyperactive church spun its wheels in unproductive activity.

Laodicea had wandered furthest. It had turned the faith completely upside down, taking on worldly values, baptizing them, and pretending that made them Christian. Again, a failing in behavior stemmed from a breakdown of careful thought.

For the most part, problems faced by the inland churches arose from the entrenched societies of their cities: craft guilds, popular temples, families of great prestige and influence who set the social standards and had done so for generations. Old wealth and power, in spite of the new Roman control, still set much of the stage on which the early church played its first roles in history. And the church had trouble with them as much as it did with new wealth and power. It is difficult to feel secure with a new faith when one is surrounded with contrary institutions that seem to have stood the test of time.

The Letter to Sardis (3:1-6)

Sardis was an ancient city that had risen in splendor in 560 B.C. and had been in gradual decline ever since. It had great wealth, and its wealth made it irresponsible. Sardis had military might, and that might made it overconfident. Twice, despite its magnificent strategic position, enemies had scaled its walls at night and conquered the city. The guards, foolishly incautious, had left their posts.

John knows that history. He reminds the Christians at Sardis that his message comes from the one who holds seven spirits in his hand. In the early church, as in Judaism, the spirits are viewed as the sources by which God gives life and enlivens the living. The reference to the spirits contrasts with the city of Sardis and its church, who *have the reputation* (CEB; *name,* NRSV) *of being alive* but are dead.

Christians living in a city that had been twice captured by enemies in the dark of night would surely understand allusions to God's coming *like a thief in the night*. They must remain alert and watchful. Part of watchfulness is remembering. The Greek word for *remembering* means more than to entertain a past event in one's mind. It means to let that remembrance bear on one's behavior.

Robes of white symbolize holiness. They will be worn by those whose names remain in the book of life. Ancient cities used registration books to certify those who had the rights of citizenship. In this case, John reminds those who remain faithful that their names fill not an earthly register but God's book of life. In the soft and spoiled city of Sardis, the eventual and true victors are those who awaken, remember, and remain watchful.

John's reference to the *book of life* would have kindled recollections of different sorts among the Jewish and Greek Christians. Jewish religion used the notion of official lists in several ways. As early as Exodus, there are records of official lists and of registrars to make them. Those lists determined who could share in the community's goods. One punishment greatly feared would be to have one's name removed from the list. It meant no more access to food and supplies—almost certainly death.

The *book of life* gradually came to mean not the list of citizens of the nation, but of those who were citizens in God's kingdom. And, again, to have one's name removed from the book is a grim sentence. But the more positive message is the one conveyed here: Those whose religion deprives them of the rights of earthly citizenship have their names inscribed else-where. They are not forgotten.

Greek and Roman cities of John's time also kept lists. All new citizens were entered into the records. And when citizens violated the laws suffi-ciently, their names were erased. That erasure may have been the fate of those exiled to Patmos with John. In this case, a name on the book gave one the rights of citizenship and the protection of the community. Loss of those rights cost one, if not his life, very likely his livelihood.

Christians of either Greek or Jewish background, then, would know the deprivation of losing their place in the book. Those in Sardis needed especially to think of that. They had, in effect, traded one book for the other. Inscribing their names so willingly on the registry of secular ways had erased them from the book of life.

The white garments promised those who endure draw attention also to two different notions. Among the Romans, the typical holiday robe was white. On a day celebrating a military triumph, white was the universal color. Dark-colored robes were worn as signs of sorrow and mourning.

If white celebrates the Roman military conqueror, John can make it celebrate the Christian conqueror—the one who overcomes temptation. For him, white stands for purity, not worldly power. He will, later in the book, again depict the martyrs and the other faithful dressed in white.

Once more, John shows how to take the familiar events about him and rescript them to speak in a new voice, with a new meaning. The military parade transforms into a pageant in heaven. The book of registry becomes a book of life. The conqueror becomes not one who overwhelms others but one who overcomes temptation.

The Letter to Laodicea (3:14-22)

Laodicea was one of the richest commercial cities in the world. It contained a famous medical school, a widely-known clothing and wool industry, and a vast banking enterprise. Among its many medical products, Laodicea manufactured a highly regarded eye salve.

In the presence of this wealth, popular clothing industry, and remarkable eye medicine, John finds a church that has become spiritually poor, naked, and blind. Its affluence has closed its eyes to its own mediocrity. Neither hot nor cold, the Laodiceans' lukewarm religion has spoiled the church's savor.

John calls the Laodicean church *poor*, as he had called the church at Smyrna poor. He uses the same strong Greek word in both cases. Here, however, it does not refer to matters of wealth but to matters of the spirit. The Christians at Smyrna had almost no possessions at all; the Laodiceans possessed almost no faith at all. Christ calls the Laodicean church to recover its self-understanding, to see that it must define itself by what comes from Christ, not by what comes from the glamour of wealth that surrounds it. Christ's gold and garments and salve alone mark and heal the faithful.

Those who hear and respond to God's call will find themselves chastised. (Chastisement combines the two notions of punishment and being made pure.) But they will also find themselves surprisingly transformed into hosts; and Christ himself will come to dine with them. The Greek word translated *eat* may also be translated to *sup,* and is the same word used in the phrase *the Lord's Supper*. It means a long and intimate meal together.

The conquerors, again, are not those who wear crowns like the rulers of the secular world, but those who see the race through to the end. Their crowns connote victory after endurance, not royal power.

The Message of Revelation 2:18–3:22

The letters written to the churches of Asia Minor are meant for all churches. The messages to them spoke both to the specific problems of each church and to the church in general.

The churches in the inland cities endured some trials in common with those on the coast. But they also faced some that were peculiar to themselves. To them, John sent messages of both general and particular significance. Chief among those messages are the following:

§ Christians will face hard times and will also be severely tempted in good times.

§ God loves and will strengthen the faithful.

§ Not all danger arises from outside the church; distortions of belief and behavior can emerge from within as well.

§ God knows the special circumstances of each church and Christian.

§ Immorality is not simply a matter of behavior. It can also stem from a lack of careful thought about the beliefs of the church.

§ Those who endure in faith will be rewarded by God.

§ Even those outside of the church can learn to worship in truth and find favor with God.

§ Christians should be watchful for the coming of God.

October 31, 2021

Lesson 9
COVENANT RENEWAL

Focal Passage
Deuteronomy 29:10-29

Background Text
Deuteronomy 29

Purpose
To let Moses show us the need for, and the shape of, covenant renewal
for us today

Summary
We tend to think of the church as the fulfillment of God's plan
insofar as Gentiles are invited into the assembly. Nevertheless, we
know we frequently miss the mark. In this study, we look back to
God's covenant with the Israelites and the pattern for covenant renewal
laid forth in the Book of Deuteronomy. Should we think of the
covenant described as the new covenant in the New Testament as a
covenant renewal? What lessons for covenant renewal might we learn
from our study of Deuteronomy 29? What would it mean if we were to
think of every time God's people gather in worship as a time of
covenant renewal?

SCRIPTURE
Deuteronomy 29:10-29

[10]Right now, all of you are in the presence of the LORD your God—the leaders of your tribes,[a] your elders, and your officials, all the Israelite males, [11]your children, your wives, and the immigrants who live with you in your camp, the ones who chop your wood and those who draw your water—[12]ready to enter into the LORD your God's covenant and into the agreement that the LORD your God is making with you right now. [13]That means the Lord will make you his own people right now—he will be your God just as he promised you and just as he swore to our ancestors: to Abraham, Isaac, and Jacob. [14]But I'm not making this covenant and this agreement with you alone [15]but also with those standing here with us right now before the LORD our God, and also with those who aren't here with us right now.

[16]You know firsthand how we used to live in Egypt and how we passed right through the nations that you passed through. [17]You saw the horrific things, the filthy idols of wood and stone, silver and gold, that they had with them. [18]Make sure there isn't any one among you right now—male or female, clan or tribe—whose mind is turning from being with the LORD our God in favor of going to serve these nations' gods. Make sure there isn't any root among you that is sprouting poison and bitterness. [19]When that kind of person hears the words of this agreement, they congratulate themselves, thinking: I'll be fine even though I insist on being stubborn. This would cause something wet to dry up and become like something parched.[b] [20]The LORD won't be willing to forgive that kind of person; instead, the LORD's anger and passion will smolder against that person. Every curse written in this scroll will stretch out over them, and the LORD will wipe out their name from under the heavens. [21]Out of all Israel's tribes, the LORD will single them out for disaster in compliance with all the

covenant curses that are written in this Instruction scroll.

²²Future generations, your children after you, or foreigners from distant lands will say: Look[c] at all that land's plagues and the sicknesses that the LORD laid on it! ²³Look at all its land burned by sulfur and salt, unsuitable for planting, unable to grow or produce any vegetation, as devastated as Sodom and Gomorrah, Admah and Zeboiim, which the LORD devastated in anger and wrath! ²⁴Indeed, all nations will ask: Why did the LORD do this to this land? What led to this terrible display of anger? ²⁵They will deduce: It was because those people abandoned the covenant of the LORD, their ancestors' God, which he made with them when he brought them out of Egypt. ²⁶They followed other gods,

serving them and worshipping them—other gods that they hadn't experienced before and that the Lord hadn't designated for them. ²⁷Then the LORD's anger burned against that land, and he brought against it every curse written in this scroll. ²⁸The LORD ripped them off their land in anger, wrath, and great fury. He threw them into other lands, and that's how things still stand today.

²⁹The secret things belong to the LORD our God. The revealed things belong to us and to our children forever: to keep all the words of this covenant.

---

[a] Deuteronomy 29:10 LXX, Syr; MT *your leaders your tribes*
[b] Deuteronomy 29:19 Heb uncertain; perhaps the agricultural imagery of 29:18 is continued here or the terms are metaphors for human states.
[c] Deuteronomy 29:22 Or *after they see*

COMMENTARY
Deuteronomy 29

Deuteronomy 28–30 contain the third and final sermon of Moses to the people before they cross the Jordan into the Promised Land. First, however, Moses concludes his earlier sermon begun in chapter 5. Then he proceeds to exhort the people to obey the covenant made with God, and warns them of the punishment they will incur if they do not obey.

A Description of the Covenant (29:1-29)

This chapter begins Moses' third sermon (the three sermons are found in chapters 1–4; 5–28; and 29–30). Verse 1 serves as an introduction to the next two chapters. In the Hebrew text, this verse is the last verse in the previous chapter.

This introduction mentions a covenant made in Moab, in addition to the one made earlier at Horeb (Sinai). Usually, the covenant mentioned here is a renewal of the earlier covenant. This covenant in Moab is not mentioned anywhere else in the Old Testament.

Verses 2-9 are a recital of God's accomplishments in history, beginning with the deliverance from oppression in Egypt, moving through the wilderness experience and the defeat of Sihon and Og, to the taking of their territory east of the Jordan River.

Verses 10-15 are an invitation to accept the covenant; these verses repeat the summons given in 26:16-19.

Verses 16-28 continue Moses' speech about what may happen if the people reject the covenant at some time in the future. First, if an individual turns away from God and toward the gods of other nations, God would *blot out* his or her name (verse 20), in addition to other calamities that would come upon the people as a whole. Then, when later generations question the origin of these calamities, they will be told they are the result of the Israelites' worshipping other gods.

The phrase *this book* occurs several times in this passage (verses 20, 21, 27, and 29). The phrase refers to the Book of Deuteronomy itself. The references indicate that these particular verses are a later addition to the book.

The Message of Deuteronomy 29

§ Blessings and curses are both options for the Israelites, depending on their response to the covenant.

§ Events in the future (such as the Babylonian exile) are seen as a direct result of the people's disregard for the covenant.

§ Disobedience of the commandments will have disastrous results; obedience will bring a life of peace and prosperity.

§ God's actions in the past on Israel's behalf are proof that God will continue to act on behalf of the chosen people in the future.

UNIT 3
November 2021

THE FELLOWSHIP OF THE TABLE

Introduction to the Unit

Once one enters the church through baptism, the central identity marker for membership in the church is participation in the Lord's Supper. The opening of God's people to both Jews and Greeks, men and women, masters and slaves required people previously unaccustomed to eating together to sit down at a common table. When we look at the Gospel narratives, we see Jesus modeling open table fellowship. In this unit, we will look at the significance of the practice of open table fellowship in the church as a sign of God's shared abundance, ministry of reconciliation, and celebration.

November 7, 2021

Lesson 10
SHARED ABUNDANCE

Focal Passage
John 6:1-15

Background Text
2 Corinthians 9:6-15

Purpose
To discover how Jesus' emphasis upon God's abundance alters our beliefs and actions as disciples

Summary
The miracle of the feeding of the multitudes is distinct to the Christian story. Other Greco-Roman narratives tell of miraculous healings and even resurrections, but nothing like this. The version of the story in John 6 is rich with nuances, pointing the significance of the meal as a sign of God's shared abundance.

SCRIPTURE
John 6:1-15

After this Jesus went across the Galilee Sea (that is, the Tiberias Sea). ²A large crowd followed him, because they had seen the miraculous signs he had done among the sick. ³Jesus went up a mountain and sat there with his disciples. [4]It was nearly time for Passover, the Jewish festival.

[5]Jesus looked up and saw the large crowd coming toward him. He asked Philip, "Where will we buy food to feed these people?" [6]Jesus said this to test him, for he already knew what he was going to do.

[7]Philip replied, "More than a half year's salary[a] worth of food wouldn't be enough for each person to have even a little bit."

[8]One of his disciples, Andrew, Simon Peter's brother, said, [9]"A youth here has five barley loaves and two fish. But what good is that for a crowd like this?"

[10]Jesus said, "Have the people sit down." There was plenty of grass there. They sat down, about five thousand of them. [11]Then Jesus took the bread. When he had given thanks, he distributed it to those who were sitting there. He did the same with the fish, each getting as much as they wanted. [12]When they had plenty to eat, he said to his disciples, "Gather up the leftover pieces, so that nothing will be wasted." [13]So they gathered them and filled twelve baskets with the pieces of the five barley loaves that had been left over by those who had eaten.

[14]When the people saw that he had done a miraculous sign, they said, "This is truly the prophet who is coming into the world." [15]Jesus understood that they were about to come and force him to be their king, so he took refuge again, alone on a mountain.

[a] John 6:7 Or *two hundred denaria*

COMMENTARY
John 6

This section records Jesus' attending Passover. This festival was held in the spring of the year. As noted with the previous festival, Jesus' activities and teachings are appropriate to Passover. Jesus feeds the large crowd, supplying life's bread; walks on the sea and quells the storms of life; and teaches about his identity as the bread of life. For the Jews, Passover centered on two general themes: God's deliverance of Israel in the *past* (through Moses), and God's promised deliverance of Israel in the *future* (through the coming Messiah). Into this situation, Jesus arrives. Through his work and teachings, he redefines Passover.

Feeding the Five Thousand (6:1-15)

The transition verses are important at the beginning of this chapter. Geographically, Jesus crosses over the water. We are reminded of the Israelites crossing the Red Sea.

Because of what has occurred in chapter 5, Jesus has a significant following. Jesus healed the diseased and, seeing the signs, the people followed him. And now, further healing signs are about to be given that suggest continued health maintenance—but only in Christ. (This is the fourth sign.)

Jesus goes up the mountain with his disciples (verse 3). This reminds us of the opening verse of the Sermon on the Mount in Matthew 5–7 or the Sermon on the Plain in Luke 6–7. Something very important is about to happen. The stage is set. Jesus is at the center of the scene. The disciples are next in order, gathered around Jesus. Then come the masses.

The Feast of Unleavened Bread (Passover) intimated many significant things for the Jews. This was the bread that sustained the Israelites during their deliverance from Egypt (Exodus 12). In like manner, Jesus is about to become the *unleavened* (sinless) bread that will sustain all humanity during their deliverance from sin and rebellion. The unleavened bread of Passover is the bread of *affliction* (Deuteronomy 16:1-8). As it helps the Israelites remember their past, so Christ—the true bread—will help humanity remember their daily dependence upon God.

Jesus sees the crowds *coming toward him* (verse 5) and immediately inquires about their basic needs. His overriding concern is for the sustenance, upbuilding, and general maintenance of those who would follow him.

Jesus' question to Philip is exact: Where shall we buy bread, so that these people may eat? The question is full of Old Testament overtones and parallels when compared with Israel's murmurings in the wilderness (Numbers 11). Moses asks God a similar question (Numbers 11:13). In Moses' situation, the people grumbled, as do the Jews after Jesus refers to himself as the *bread from heaven* (verses 41-43). Jesus teaches about *manna* (verse 31), referring to the Moses incident. In both cases, bread is the sufficient substitute for flesh. Finally, there is a reference to "possible" fish (Numbers 11:22) and to the supplying of fish by the little boy in John's Gospel (verse 9). The parallels seem to suggest that, in the past, God supplied Israel's needs. But now, in Christ, humanity's needs are supplied completely and forever.

Then we read that Jesus is simply testing Philip. The emphasis of the verse is on Jesus. Although Philip is *encouraged* or tested in his faith, Jesus knows what has to be done. He knows his mission. He knows the work he has to accomplish. Philip, thinking on a different (materialistic) level—as with Nicodemus and the woman at the well—simply responds by saying the cash is not available (verse 7). The amount of money referred to by Philip would be equivalent to two hundred days' wages, an amazing sum.

Then Andrew (Simon Peter's brother) introduces a wonderful change in the setting. It is not unimportant that a *boy* has a lunch—a lad similar to the one healed earlier (4:49). The servant of the bread of life is a young lad or a child. The innocence, wonder, and trust of the child are the very characteristics associated with those who would follow Jesus. Further, barley loaves are the food of the poor (*the poor in spirit*), those who need to be healed. Dried fish is a normal food, although eventually a fish became the sign of the church. As the Gospel states, Andrew is not enthusiastic about the advantage of this little lunch in relation to the masses of hungry people.

Jesus takes command. He tells the disciples to have the people sit down—perhaps not an easy task, considering the masses and possible confusion. In the normal Jewish manner, only the men are numbered. Undoubtedly, on the basis of the lad himself, women and children are present. How Jesus gets the lunch is not stated, but we can assume one of the disciples (probably Andrew) asks the boy if the master or *rabbi* can make use of his little parcel of food.

Jesus gives thanks, or says a prayer, over the food, and the people are filled. The Greek word used for Jesus' *thanks* is *eucharistein* or *eucharist*. This later came to mean the sacrament of the Lord's Supper. Hence, the breaking of the bread and drinking of the cup at the Last Supper carry the meaning of *thanksgiving*, *blessing*, and *communion*. The fact that the people who came to Jesus were filled implies the sufficiency of Christ. He is the fulfilling of God's free choice of love and fellowship with humanity. Nothing more is needed.

The disciples are then commanded to gather up what remains so nothing is lost. This gathering up is similar to the gathering of the manna in the wilderness (Exodus 16:16-20). But unlike the manna of old, this "manna" (Christ) in the "wilderness" (of this lost world) must not be lost. The mission must be fulfilled.

In the fulfilling of the mission, when the Son or Lamb is sacrificed, God's costly grace is not to be wasted or mocked or to return to him void (see Jesus' instructions to the seventy, Luke 10:1-12). The disciples fill twelve baskets. Here is a reference to the remnant of Israel or the twelve new tribes of Israel, the body of Christ.

Jesus is immediately identified as a prophet (verse 14). Perhaps he is identified as a Moses-type prophet (see verse 31) who will do great things for the people of God. They so misunderstand his mission that they seek to make him king (verse 15). So, Jesus withdraws to a mountain for meditation and communion with the Father. The sign of the feeding was meant to explain how *the one* (his identity) feeds the man; how this *one act* (his mission) in time is an act for all humanity for eternity. Jesus, then, is the bread of life that overcomes the troubled world.

The Message of John 6

In this Passover feast, the emphasis falls on Jesus as the bread of life and Jesus' power over chaos. At the previous Passover, he cleansed the Temple. On the next Passover, he will offer himself as a sacrifice for the many. So, we see a movement from getting the *temple* (of his body) ready to now establishing the new element (the unleavened bread) and rationale (defeating the seas of chaos), to finally reconstituting this entire Jewish festival that celebrates God's deliverance of Israel.

During this second Passover, Jesus is established as the bread of life. He is a prophetic Moses figure of the past, and manna, the shewbread that was expected to be a sign of the new Messiah's arrival. He is the bread provided by God to reconcile humanity to God. But he is also the future bread of life (the bread of the Lord's Supper). He is the new Passover that will allow those present (the five thousand) and all pilgrims of the festival to feast on him. They will rely upon his soon-to-be-accomplished work (the next Passover) of reconciliation.

Lesson 11
A MEAL OF RECONCILIATION

Focal Passage
1 Samuel 25:2-39

Background Text
1 Samuel 25

Purpose
To understand how the experience of a meal can overcome human differences and lead to grace

Summary
Sitting down at table with one another is a sign of friendship and trust, so it should be no surprise that food often plays a central role in stories of reconciliation. When Nabal (whose name means "fool") refuses to help David, Abigail seeks to smooth over the tensions with a meal. Her story invites us to think about the significance of the Lord's Supper as a meal of reconciliation.

SCRIPTURE
1 Samuel 25:2-39

²There was a man in Maon who did business in Carmel. He was a very important man and owned three thousand sheep and one thousand

goats. At that time, he was shearing his sheep in Carmel. [3]The man's name was Nabal, and his wife's name was Abigail. She was an intelligent and attractive woman, but her husband was a hard man who did evil things. He was a Calebite.

[4]While in the wilderness, David heard that Nabal was shearing his sheep. [5]So David sent ten servants, telling them, "Go up to Carmel. When you get to Nabal, greet him for me. [6]Say this to him: 'Peace to you,[a] your household, and all that is yours! [7]I've heard that you are now shearing sheep. As you know, your shepherds were with us in the wilderness.[b] We didn't mistreat them. Moreover, the whole time they were at Carmel, nothing of theirs went missing. [8]Ask your servants; they will tell you the same. So please receive these young men favorably, because we've come on a special day. Please give whatever you have on hand to your servants and to your son David.'"

[9]When David's young men arrived, they said all this to Nabal on David's behalf. Then they waited. [10]But Nabal answered David's servants, "Who is David? Who is Jesse's son? There are all sorts of slaves running away from their masters these days. [11]Why should I take my bread, my water, and the meat I've butchered for my shearers and give it to people who came here from who knows where?" [12]So David's young servants turned around and went back the way they came. When they arrived, they reported every word of this to David.

[13]Then David said to his soldiers, "All of you, strap on your swords!" So each of them strapped on their swords, and David did the same. Nearly four hundred men went up with David. Two hundred men remained back with the supplies.

[14]One of Nabal's servants told his wife Abigail, "David sent messengers from the wilderness to greet our master, but he just yelled at them. [15]But the men were very good to us and didn't mistreat us. Nothing of ours went missing the whole time we were out with them

in the fields. [16]In fact, the whole time we were with them, watching our sheep, they were a protective wall around us both night and day. [17]Think about that and see what you can do, because trouble is coming for our master and his whole household. But he's such a despicable person no one can speak to him."

[18]Abigail quickly took two hundred loaves of bread, two skins of wine, five sheep ready for cooking, five seahs[c] of roasted grain, one hundred raisin cakes, and two hundred fig cakes. She loaded all this on donkeys [19]and told her servants, "Go on ahead of me. I'll be right behind you." But she didn't tell her husband Nabal.

[20]As she was riding her donkey, going down a trail on the hillside, David and his soldiers appeared, descending toward her, and she met up with them. [21]David had just been saying, "What a waste of time—guarding all this man's stuff in the wilderness so that nothing of his went missing! He has repaid me evil instead of good! [22]May God deal harshly with me, David,[d] and worse still if I leave alive even one single one who urinates on a wall[e] belonging to him come morning!"

[23]When Abigail saw David, she quickly got off her donkey and fell facedown before him, bowing low to the ground. [24]She fell at his feet and said, "Put the blame on me, my master! But please let me, your servant, speak to you directly. Please listen to what your servant has to say. [25]Please, my master, pay no attention to this despicable man Nabal. He's exactly what his name says he is! His name means fool,[f] and he is foolish![g] But I myself, your servant, didn't see the young men that you, my master, sent. [26]I pledge, my master, as surely as the LORD lives and as you live, that the LORD has held you back from bloodshed and taking vengeance into your own hands! But now let your enemies and those who seek to harm my master be exactly like Nabal! [27]Here is a gift, which your servant has brought to my master. Please let it be given to the young men who follow you, my master.

[28]Please forgive any offense by your servant. The LORD will definitely make an enduring dynasty for my master because my master fights the LORD's battles, and nothing evil will be found in you throughout your lifetime. [29]If someone chases after you and tries to kill you, my master, then your life will be bound up securely in the bundle of life[h] by the LORD your God, but he will fling away your enemies' lives as from the pouch of a sling. [30]When the LORD has done for my master all the good things he has promised you, and has installed you as Israel's leader, [31]don't let this be a blot or burden on my master's conscience, that you shed blood needlessly or that my master took vengeance into his own hands. When the LORD has done good things for my master, please remember your servant."

[32]David said to Abigail, "Bless the LORD God of Israel, who sent you to meet me today! [33]And bless you and your good judgment for preventing me from shedding blood and taking vengeance into my own hands today! [34]Otherwise, as surely as the LORD God of Israel lives— the one who kept me from hurting you—if you hadn't come quickly and met up with me, there wouldn't be one single one who urinates on a wall left come morning." [35]Then David accepted everything she had brought for him. "Return home in peace," he told her. "Be assured that I've heard your request and have agreed to it."

[36]When Abigail got back home to Nabal, he was throwing a party fit for a king in his house. Nabal was in a great mood and very drunk, so Abigail didn't tell him anything until daybreak. [37]In the morning, when Nabal was sober, his wife told him everything. Nabal's heart failed inside him, and he became like a stone. [38]About ten days later, the LORD struck Nabal, and he died.

[39]When David heard that Nabal was dead, he said, "Bless the LORD, who has rendered a verdict regarding Nabal's insult to me and who kept me, his servant, from doing something evil! The LORD has

brought Nabal's evil down on his own head." Then David sent word to Abigail, saying that he would take her as his wife.

---

[a] 1 Samuel 25:6 Heb uncertain

[b] 1 Samuel 25:7 LXX, Syr; MT lacks *in the wilderness.*

[c] 1 Samuel 25:18 One seah is approximately seven and a half quarts.

[d] 1 Samuel 25:22 LXX; MT *with David's enemies*

[e] 1 Samuel 25:22 Descriptive phrase meaning "a male"; also in 25:34

[f] 1 Samuel 25:25 Heb *nabal*

[g] 1 Samuel 25:25 Heb *nebalah*

[h] 1 Samuel 25:29 Or *bundle of the living;* Heb uncertain; perhaps a tied-up scroll (cf Exod 32:32-33; Ps 69:28; Isa 8:16)

COMMENTARY

1 Samuel 25:2-39

This passage is preceded by the death of Samuel, an important leader in early Israelite history. Five chapters later, the death of Saul, another important figure, occurs.

David's Courtship of Abigail (25:1-44)

The opening verse of chapter 25 is a notice of Samuel's death. In view of Samuel's national fame and prominence, the brevity of the remark is surprising. This notice is repeated in 28:3, to set the scene for Saul's seance with Samuel.

This delightful story tells how David acquires two members of his harem, Abigail and Ahinoam. The writer here resumes the pro-monarchy source left at 23:14 following David's escape at Keilah. David is the leader of a renegade band of soldiers and furnishes protection to local landowners in return for payment. David appears to have left his fortress at Adullam and is currently operating in the area close to Hebron—namely, the regions of Ziph and Maon.

Verse 1b states that David went to the wilderness of Paran; this reading follows the Hebrew text. The Greek version reads Maon, as in verse 2. Due to the considerable distance of Paran from Maon, as well as from Ziph, the Greek reading seems more appropriate.

Nabal, whose name means *foolish*, is a wealthy shepherd who belongs to the Calebite tribe (Numbers 13; 14). Unfortunately, he has a mean disposition.

The scene opens with Nabal conducting a sheepshearing festival which is partly work and partly celebration. David has been serving as a protector for Nabal and his valuable flocks. David doubtless served also in a similar capacity for other residents of the area. But when David asks politely for provisions as payment for his service, Nabal refuses and asks, "Who is the son of Jesse?" The reference to *many servants* who are *breaking away* indicates the turbulent and uneasy political situation in Judah at this time, hosting frequent raids from the Philistines, the Amalekites, and others. David's sense of outrage (verse 13) is understandable, considering Nabal's insult.

One of Nabal's servants describes the dangerous situation to Abigail. Probably he fears for his own life and hopes proper intercession can be made. The servant verifies David's claim that Nabal's possessions have in fact remained safe and undisturbed under his protection. Thus, Nabal's response is not only insulting to David but also unjustified. David's threat (verse 22) must strike terror into the hearts of Nabal's servants.

Abigail responds by hastily gathering lavish provisions and sending them immediately to David, following shortly behind herself. Her gracious and courteous manner impresses David greatly. She argues that David should reconsider his threat and should do no harm to Nabal. After all, the man is a fool, as his name implies. David needs to remain guiltless before God and not stoop to this act of revenge. She reminds David that his life is closely guarded by God (verse 29) and that Nabal poses no serious threat to him. Therefore, he must not take matters into his own hands and replace God by slaying Nabal himself, for this act would usurp the prerogative of God (verses 28-31). This was precisely Saul's sin when he blessed the troops at Gilgal (13:8-9). Bloodguilt is inappropriate for Israel's next king.

David agrees to her proposal and accepts her gifts. Abigail returns home. At the proper moment, she tells Nabal. Almost instantly, he suffers a fatal stroke (verse 37) and dies shortly afterwards. David then proposes marriage to Abigail, and she accepts. David has acquired not only a beautiful and intelligent wife but considerable wealth and land as well. He has extended his influence in the southern territory of Judah. Further strengthening his ties in the south, he marries another princess from Jezreel, a Judahite (not a northern city), Ahinoam by name. By this time, Saul has already given Michal, David's first wife, to another man. Once again, divine providence has halted David from making a tragic mistake and has rewarded him with a perfectly-suited mate.

The Message of 1 Samuel 25

David was open to divine guidance. He has good reason to avenge Nabal's insult, yet he listens to Abigail's wise words urging restraint. She tells him to avoid incurring bloodguilt and that God, not David, will take care of Nabal. In an incident that follows, David refuses to allow Abishai to kill Saul and explains that God will deal with the king. Later, too, David consults the Lord in the matter of revenge against the Amalekites (30:7). David's faith in soliciting divine guidance distinguishes him from King Saul.

Lesson 12
COMMUNION CONNECTIONS

Focal Passage
1 Corinthians 11:17-34

Background Text
Luke 22:14-20

Purpose
To understand how taking the Lord's Supper can produce a powerful experience of unity within a diverse congregation

Summary
Meals are times to get together to sustain the identity as families and friendship circles. Paul's teaching about the Lord's Supper and the words of constitution he shares remind us not only that the meal constitutes the community but what sort of community we are to be.

SCRIPTURE
1 Corinthians 11:17-34

[17]Now I don't praise you as I give the following instruction because when you meet together, it does more harm than good. [18]First of all, when you meet together as a church, I hear that there are divisions among you, and I partly believe it. [19]It's necessary that there are

groups among you, to make it clear who is genuine. [20]So when you get together in one place, it isn't to eat the Lord's meal. [21]Each of you goes ahead and eats a private meal. One person goes hungry while another is drunk. [22]Don't you have houses to eat and drink in? Or do you look down on God's churches and humiliate those who have nothing? What can I say to you? Will I praise you? No, I don't praise you in this.

[23]I received a tradition from the Lord, which I also handed on to you: on the night on which he was betrayed, the Lord Jesus took bread. [24]After giving thanks, he broke it and said, "This is my body, which is for you; do this to remember me." [25]He did the same thing with the cup, after they had eaten, saying, "This cup is the new covenant in my blood. Every time you drink it, do this to remember me." [26]Every time you eat this bread and drink this cup, you broadcast the death of the Lord until he comes.

[27]This is why those who eat the bread or drink the cup of the Lord inappropriately will be guilty of the Lord's body and blood. [28]Each individual should test himself or herself, and eat from the bread and drink from the cup in that way. [29]Those who eat and drink without correctly understanding the body are eating and drinking their own judgment. [30]Because of this, many of you are weak and sick, and quite a few have died. [31]But if we had judged ourselves, we wouldn't be judged. [32]However, we are disciplined by the Lord when we are judged so that we won't be judged and condemned along with the whole world. [33]For these reasons, my brothers and sisters, when you get together to eat, wait for each other. [34]If some of you are hungry, they should eat at home so that getting together doesn't lead to judgment. I will give directions about the other things when I come.

COMMENTARY
1 Corinthians 11:17-34

The central activity of the believers at Corinth was worship. This section of chapter 11 focuses on the celebration of the Lord's Supper.

Practicing the Lord's Supper (11:17-34)

Paul indicates his concern about this issue with his opening words. Paul cannot *commend* or *praise* them for this issue. He would like to, but he cannot. In fact, based upon reports he has received, the believers at Corinth are spiritually hindered by their assembly for worship. This bold assertion suggests Paul's deep concern over the manner in which they celebrate the Communion meal at worship. For Paul, the Lord's Supper is the key element in worship. The information Paul has received has yet to be verified. But it is such a scandalous report that Paul says he partly believes it. No one would invent such a report. First of all, there are divisions or diverse group attitudes among the believers. The very fact that these different attitudes or divisions exist suggests that at least some are genuine in their faith, clinging to Christ alone. With this state of affairs, the Corinthian believers are certainly not coming together as one body or fellowship in Christ when they think they are eating the Lord's Supper. Because of their divisions, they are not honoring but slandering Christ.

What are these different divisions? The divisions include differing attitudes about the Supper based on class distinction and possibly kosher foods. The believers are not eating the Lord's Supper because they do not hold to ceremony. Rather, each person is eating as he or she wishes. Some people are going hungry because others eat everything; others drink so much, they are drunk in the assembly of worship.

Having repeated what he has heard, Paul's immediate response is disbelief: *What!* Can this be? (verse 22). People should take these attitudes about the Lord's Supper and practice them in their own homes. These attitudes are not right for Christ's church in worship. And Paul will not commend them for practicing the Lord's Supper because these very attitudes suggest they are not communing together and they are not communing in the Lord.

Paul's previous instruction about the Lord's Supper was directly from the Lord. How Paul received this tradition from the Lord is not clear. Was Paul an eyewitness of Jesus and his ministry? Did Paul receive this information from one who was an eyewitness? one of the original disciples? Did Paul receive this information on the Damascus road? As we noted earlier, Paul was probably not an eyewitness of Jesus or he would have argued this in support of his apostleship. It is most likely Paul received this information from one of the original disciples and then had his understanding further confirmed by the living Lord.

In any case, Paul gives the Corinthians a summary of what he has taught them in the past. These words quoting Jesus form the oldest written tradition known for instituting the Lord's Supper. The Gospels of Matthew (26:26-29), Mark (14:22-25), and Luke (22:14-20) follow Paul's words, suggesting that this tradition comes from the disciples. We should recall that Paul's statements describe Jesus' action with the disciples on the night before Passover. The Passover festival celebrated Israel's deliverance from Egypt. The celebration centered on a sacrificial lamb that was offered to God. In this context, Jesus' words take on a deep meaning which the Corinthians seem to have forgotten in the midst of all their infighting and silly practices. The Supper is for the *remembrance* of Christ and his work; it is a memorial that recalls his lamb-type sacrifice that delivers humanity from rebellion and self-destruction.

The cup carries the same significance as the bread. As the bread represents Christ's body, so the cup represents the new covenant sealed in his blood. The bread (Christ's body) represents the main meal; the cup is the drink that confirms and finalizes the meal. Thus, the cup seals the covenant established by the sacrifice of Christ's flesh (see Exodus 24:8; Jeremiah 31:31-34). Paul concludes by explaining the purpose of this memorial.

Whenever the Corinthian believers share in the Lord's Supper, they bear witness to the truth of Christ. And they are called to be witnesses until *he comes* (verse 26; 15:23-25).

Having stated the rumored practices of the Corinthians and the correct meaning of the Lord's Supper, Paul makes an obvious conclusion. The person who wrongly practices the Lord's Supper is guilty of making Christ's sacrifice for the deliverance of humanity null and void. Do not lapse into bad habits. This is the center of worship. Approach it cautiously by first examining the self so the Supper will truly be a witness to the living and resurrected Christ. But if a person partakes of the Lord's Supper without realizing that the food signifies the body and blood of Christ, that person brings judgment upon himself or herself—eternal judgment.

This eternal judgment works itself out in practical ways. In Paul's day, it was thought that demons were the cause of sickness, mental illness, and sometimes death (10:20). There were those present in the fellowship who were *weak and ill* (NRSV; *sick,* CEB). Some even had died or *fallen asleep.* Paul uses this fact as a warning that the Lord's Supper be practiced properly and correctly. If believers perceive the true spiritual meaning of the Supper and examine themselves in Christ before partaking, they cannot be *judged* because they will be right with God in the covenant of Christ. But then again, Paul seems to add almost as an afterthought, when God does judge us, God disciplines us so we will not fall (verse 32).

Then Paul concludes his instruction and comments. His concern is that they *wait for one another*. Eat the meal together as a fellowship, remembering Christ's life and work. If it is food you want, eat at home. Otherwise, you destroy the meaning of the Lord's Supper. And there are other problems in the Corinthian practice of the Lord's Supper that he will give directions about later. But this more important error of division and attitude had to be dealt with immediately.

November 28, 2021

Lesson 13
COME TO THE BANQUET
(THE FIRST SUNDAY OF ADVENT)

Focal Passage
Isaiah 25:6-10a; 55:1-3

Background Text
Isaiah 55

Purpose
To hear and accept God's invitation to abundant life as we begin our
Advent journey

Summary
In Isaiah's account of the day of the Lord when all the nations gather
on God's holy mountain, God provides the nations with a royal
banquet. Feasting is a central feature of our celebration of the
coming of our King at Christmas. This passage reminds us that meals
are central to celebration, and that all are invited and welcomed to
God's banquet.

SCRIPTURE
Isaiah 25:6-10a

[6]On this mountain,
   the LORD of heavenly forces will prepare for all peoples
      a rich feast, a feast of choice wines,
   of select foods rich in flavor,
   of choice wines well refined.
[7]He will swallow up on this mountain the veil that is veiling all peoples,
   the shroud enshrouding all nations.
[8]He will swallow up death[a] forever. The LORD God will wipe tears from every face;

he will remove his people's disgrace from off the whole earth,
   for the LORD has spoken.
[9]They will say on that day,
"Look! This is our God,
   for whom we have waited—
   and he has saved us!
This is the LORD, for whom we have waited;
      let's be glad and rejoice in his salvation!"
[10]The LORD's hand will indeed rest on this mountain.

———————————————
[a] Isaiah 25:8 Heb *Maveth*

Isaiah 55:1-3

All of you who are thirsty, come to the water!
Whoever has no money, come, buy food and eat!
Without money, at no cost, buy wine and milk!
[2]Why spend money for what isn't food,
   and your earnings for what doesn't satisfy?
Listen carefully to me and eat what is good;
   enjoy the richest of feasts.
[3]Listen and come to me;
   listen, and you will live.
I will make an everlasting covenant with you,
   my faithful loyalty to David.

COMMENTARY
Isaiah 25:6-10a

Chapters 24–27 of the Book of Isaiah are usually called the *Isaiah Apocalypse*. Their content is primarily eschatological (relating to events at the end of time). Various kinds of prophetic literature are found in these chapters, such as apocalyptic poetry, eschatological prophecies, oracles of judgment, and oracles of salvation. Isaiah 25:6-12 is an eschatological oracle.

Most commentators agree that the Isaiah Apocalypse was not the work of the prophet Isaiah. Various suggestions have been made for the date of this section. Whereas the prophet Isaiah is most often concerned with the judgment God is about to bring upon Judah, the events spoken of in chapters 24–27 are on a worldwide scale. Concern for the events that will take place at the end of time is characteristic of the theology of later Judaism, perhaps dating these chapters to 400 or 300 B.C.

Many of the prophecies in these chapters concern a certain city whose identity is uncertain. Commentators have suggested such cities as Carthage, Babylon, and Samaria, but no one knows for certain. That is unfortunate, since the identification of the city might tell us something about the origin and date of these prophecies.

Eschatological Oracles (25:6-12)

In this section, future salvation is described and celebrated for other nations as well as for Israel. *This mountain* means Mount Zion in Jerusalem. At the future time of salvation, God will prepare a feast for all those who make pilgrimage to Jerusalem. The detailed description in verse 6 makes the point that the best possible feast will be prepared for the nations. The *shroud*, or *veil*, mentioned in verse 7 presumably means the veil of mourning. The time of mourning will be over. That idea is reinforced in verse 8.

Verses 9-10 are a thanksgiving song. The message of the song is that God will not disappoint those who have walked in hope.

Isaiah 55

Chapters 53–55 are the final three chapters in the Book of Second Isaiah, the prophet of the Babylonian Exile. They are followed by a collection of prophecies from the post-exilic period, from the hand of an anonymous prophet called Third Isaiah (chapters 56–66). Isaiah 53–55 includes the fourth servant song, a call to praise, a proclamation of salvation, a conclusion to the book, and other miscellaneous oracles.

Song of Triumph (55:1-13)

The song of triumph is a fitting way to conclude this major section in the Book of Isaiah, which began at 40:1. The song is in two parts. Verses 1-5 describe the restoration of Judah, and verses 6-13 are a kind of epilogue that summarizes the message of this prophet of the Exile.

Restoration of Judah (55:1-5)

This song is a series of imperatives, a technique often used throughout chapters 40–55. (See 51:17; 52:1, 11; 54:1.) These imperatives are different from others in these prophecies because they summon the audience to eat and drink. This kind of summons is similar to those found in the Wisdom Literature, that call persons to a banquet. (For example, see Proverbs 9:3-6.) Here, the summons is not to an actual banquet but to a restored community. The people are summoned so their souls might live (verse 30).

Verses 3-5 remind the readers of God's earlier covenant with David, in which God promised David, and Israel, steadfast love forever. Psalm 89 discusses a similar theme. When Judah is restored and the people return to dwell there, life will be so abundant that others from distant lands will come to live there too.

CPSIA information can be obtained
at www.ICGtesting.com
Printed in the USA
LVHW040459020921
696764LV00003B/105

9 781791 021467